MOVING IMAGES
haikus

Marjorie J. Levine

the three
tomatoes
The Three Tomatoes Book Publishing

Published September 2025

ISBN: 979-8-9995761-4-9
Library of Congress Control Number: 2025918301

For information address:
The Three Tomatoes Book Publishing
6 Soundview Rd.
Glen Cove, NY 11542
www.thethreetomatoespublishing.com

Cover and last page photo: courtesy of Marjorie J. Levine
Author photo: Frederick Piccarello

for all the loners who seek places to go

Viburnum MO

One sharp church steeple

Small windows with green outside

A fine safe haven.

Pottsville PA

A warm dim street lounge

A lady in pink and grey

Says goodbye to blues.

Rocky Ford CO

Cold snow is melting

As he crosses those weak tracks

Which fracture his soul.

El Reno OK

A little mailbox

With no visible address

Collects sad still dust.

Scottsbluff NE

No signs of autumn

Just an orange and brown tree

Seasons are frozen.

Riverton WY

A red bicycle

Parked under a small porch light

An empty train waits.

Pineville KY

A short ramp gives way

A small church is dwarfed by green

Green so tall he squints.

Goshen VA

A brick grocery

All boarded up and now closed

Soon a train passes.

Paducah TX

Why is there a gate

When there is not one thing there

Except a toy horse.

Clanton AL

Sweet succulent pie

Melting in her mouth like ice

And a house for sale.

Denton MT

Pink flowers in dirt

Next to two small green bunnies

And a short red chair.

Huntington TN

So many tree nests

A sewage pipe in a yard

Cats chase light blue frogs.

Elma WA

A shallow still creek

Tumbled off the rocky path

To a rusty fence.

Bellevue ID

It says hope lives there

And a warm teacup serves tea

Two wheels stop turning.

Canton NY

The American

Theater is old and stoic

A park bears witness.

Albany NY

Purple steps beckon

But lower purple balloons

Remind him to stay.

West Hickory PA

Blue and green stained glass

All under still defined clouds

A child waits to grow.

Kerrville TX

The grey old lady

Fell in love with the old man

In the quaint red car.

Lexington KY

A lumpy green chair

On a vast well lit stone porch

Waits for a new change.

Carrollton MI

Burnt orange short grass

Next to short yellow flowers

Where two new dolls dance.

Allentown PA

The lady in the

Americus Hotel waits

For her worn lover.

Los Angeles CA

Dull rain falls on stars

As tourists gather to gawk

At a showgirl's dreams.

Sedalia MO

A bike rider rides

To a brick Bed and Breakfast

His shoes turn mellow.

Ness City KS

Seven green roses

In a hanging flower pot

Make the young girl dip.

Queens NY

An old couple sees

A father hold his child

In red and thin pants.

Malverne NY

Good bye to the past

Which is a startling sad end

To a forever.

Evansville IN

With one long deep breath

The cemetery sneaks up

With misty sadness.

Camdenton MO

A brown wheelbarrow

In front of a slanted roof

Pretends to want mulch.

Bend OR

A store for cold drinks

On a vast still sandy plain

Has rusty coarse doors.

Murdo SD

A rising round sun

Above a broken white house

Waits for sweet fresh air.

Cedar City UT

Under deep turquoise

Two men sit and close the day

As mothers watch time.

Tunkhannock PA

A bright red bent tree

Under which he grew and aged

Today steals his wail.

Winnetka IL

The old is still old

Purple petals fall weakly

Days never quite age.

Wilmette IL

Even during day

A yellow streetlight is on

Through windows light melts.

Lincoln NE

He closed his brown eyes

To see unrequited love

Still under the mist.

Chicago IL

On old Dearborn Street

A grandfather's broken heart

Wept and stopped beating.

St. Paul NE

On the railroad tracks

A white car stopped for fresh air

Nothing moved in time.

Buffalo NY

The North Park Theater

Reminded her of sweet milk

And Sunday film noir.

Spokane WA

Nuanced blue whispers

On a cracked rusty light sign

Showed a way to heal.

Charlottesville VA

A camera store

A train station so bright pink

The birds saw nothing.

Elmont NY

So many grey graves

Together in life and death

One grave all alone.

Bridgeport WV

On Murphys Run Road

There is a fine covered bridge

A man bends to pray.

Clarksburg WV

Fletcher Covered Bridge

Shady and cool and just right

For two hands to bind.

Emporia KS

An old lady sighs

Yellow tall flowers now bend

Two red chairs still wait.

Ashland KS

A blue house was there

And then it was gone from view

Nothing replaced it.

Granville ND

She saw nothing there

There was not one thing to see

But peace in the air.

Olean NY

Four light green houses

All with four high steps to climb

One says "Just Be Kind."

Brooklyn NY

Old Coney Island

A wistful place to be sure

Waves recede to blips.

Brooklyn NY

On 82nd

Sadness was present

It was a default setting.

Marshalltown IA

Old Timer Tavern

A tall pot of red flowers

The day falls away.

Twin Falls ID

A settled red house

As rays of sunlight peek through

A tree stops swaying.

Douglas WY

A dark wall mural

Over an empty wood bench

Speaks of memories.

Douglas WY

A big jackalope

In a grassy town garden

She becomes obsessed.

Douglas WY

The Princess Theater

On old quaint fine N 3rd Street

A treasure indeed.

Douglas WY

I can't leave this place

It is so remarkable

Here time does stand still.

Paragould AR

Iron Mountain train

In front of a Wall of Hope

Sweet warm nostalgia.

New York NY

The Williamsburg Bridge

Is over bright blue water

Where past time stands still.

Valley Stream NY

A grassy sweet spot

Next to an old red brick school

A park lost in time.

Valley Stream NY

An old quaint red house

Was torn down and then replaced

With a huge monster.

Corning IA

She sees orange leaves

He drives a shiny new car

They face the future.

Muskogee OK

A parked light green car

Is before a lit porch light

Branches bend to dark.

Clarksdale MS

The old Paramount

On Yazoo has now fallen

Into deep despair.

El Dorado AR

A strong gazebo

With a new steel silver bench

Waits next to train tracks.

Rugby ND

He never knew her

But one day she, a stranger,

Heard he passed and stopped.

Kenilworth IL

The cold mist rises

As a tree bends to the street

A fair porch light dims.

Belle Center OH

Bickham Covered Bridge

Takes me to another side

Where roads bend to grass.

Grand Island NE

Whose eyes watch that porch

From under a spreading tree

As the cat eats crumbs.

Tucson AZ

There is a mural

With a violin player

Thinking of white clouds.

Poplar Bluff MO

A bright morning sun

Rises to shed yellow shine

A night light stays on.

Seattle WA

Many orange leaves

Collect under a bent tree

As a man sips air.

Seattle WA

A pink corner shop

Sells waffles and red flowers

Coffee hits the spot.

Harriman NY

There since forever.

An old worn cemetery

Heartbreak in all forms.

Walpack NJ

Dark green and light green

Dark red and light brown cut through

And bend to sweet change.

Farmingdale NY

As old bones decay

Time stands still in a wet fog

And dark fury drops.

Manhattan KS

The Wareham Theater

Is near a nice photo shop

Two different pictures.

Fort Yates ND

There was calm peace there

And washed wall art was so real

I stayed and stepped in.

New Holland PA

An old small greenhouse

Stands off a dusty stone road

And a flower bends.

New Holland PA

She is so stuck there

As four tired old horses

Struggle to do work.

New Holland PA

Four people stand tall

Two are little and so blurred

As their knees sink low.

Leitchfield KY

A soft round blue lake

Is near a no passing zone

A man wanders by.

Whitefish Bay WI

This is paradise

Each street painted in soft strokes

As green summer weeps.

Saskatchewan CANADA

An empty vast stretch

Was dreary until ice cream

Wet her hot pink lips.

Edmonton CANADA

A Greyhound bus left

Eyes in an old sad hotel

And later time changed.

Winnipeg CANADA

Old books and antiques

Next to an old wood theater

Music fills two ears.

Pontinha PORTUGAL

Flowers fall away

To old low strong patios

And a baby sleeps.

Madrid SPAIN

A picture of fruit

Painted on a red brick wall

As humans eat pears.

Paris FRANCE

In a side blue store

An old turquoise necklace waits

For just the right neck.

Rome ITALY

New golden sunshine

Rises from mist far away

And a cat jumps high.

Amsterdam NETHERLANDS

Two diners ponder

Still tulips falling into

A bent overpass.

Brooklyn NY

Father with baby

On a sled in ice cold snow

As time is frozen.

Martha's Vineyard MA

Those trees are old now

What happened is forgotten

The ocean still moves.

In Limbo

Old and untethered

Neither here nor there in light

A mourning dove rests.

ABOUT THE AUTHOR

Photo credit: Frederick Piccarello

Marjorie J. Levine is a retired elementary school teacher. She is the author of *Road Trips* and *Becoming Until*. *Moving Images* is her third collection of poetry. She lives alone in NYC.